U.S. ARMED FORCES

U.S. ARMY

by Allan Morey

pogo

Ideas for Parents and Teachers

Pogo Books let children practice reading informational text while introducing them to nonfiction features such as headings, labels, sidebars, maps, and diagrams, as well as a table of contents, glossary, and index.

Carefully leveled text with a strong photo match offers early fluent readers the support they need to succeed.

Before Reading

- "Walk" through the book and point out the various nonfiction features. Ask the student what purpose each feature serves.
- Look at the glossary together. Read and discuss the words.

Read the Book

- Have the child read the book independently.
- Invite him or her to list questions that arise from reading.

After Reading

- Discuss the child's questions. Talk about how he or she might find answers to those questions.
- Prompt the child to think more. Ask: Before reading this book, did you know what types of jobs U.S. Army Soldiers perform? What more would you like to learn about the U.S. Army?

Pogo Books are published by Jump!
5357 Penn Avenue South
Minneapolis, MN 55419
www.jumplibrary.com

Library of Congress Cataloging-in-Publication Data

Names: Morey, Allan, author.
Title: U.S. Army / by Allan Morey.
Description: Minneapolis, MN: Jump!, [2021]
Series: U.S. armed forces
Audience: Ages 7–10 | Audience: Grades 2–3
Identifiers: LCCN 2019044191 (print)
LCCN 2019044192 (ebook)
ISBN 9781645274216 (hardcover)
ISBN 9781645274223 (ebook)
Subjects: LCSH: United States. Army–Juvenile literature.
Classification: LCC UA25 .M675 2021 (print)
LCC UA25 (ebook) | DDC 355.00973–dc23
LC record available at https://lccn.loc.gov/2019044191
LC ebook record available at https://lccn.loc.gov/2019044192

Editor: Susanne Bushman
Designer: Molly Ballanger

Content Consultant: Specialist Kevin Ducey, U.S. Army

Specialist Kevin Ducey was a Military Police Officer stationed at Fort Drum in New York as part of the 10th Mountain Division from 1997 to 2001.

Photo Credits: U.S. Army, cover, 4, 6-7, 14–15, 16-17; DanielBendjy/iStock, 1 (foreground); turtix/Shutterstock, 1 (background); zabelin/iStock, 3; Casper1774 Studio/ Shutterstock, 5 (background); Shutterstock, 5tl, 5tm, 5tr, 5bm; grzegorz knec/Alamy, 5bl; U.S. National Guard , 5br; Oklahoma Army National Guard, 8; U.S. Army Reserve, 9; dpa picture alliance archive/Alamy, 10-11; Stocktrek Images/SuperStock, 12-13; U.S. Navy, 18; PatrickZiegler/iStock, 19; Joe Raedle/Getty, 20-21; sivapornphaiboon1983/Shutterstock, 23.

Printed in the United States of America at Corporate Graphics in North Mankato, Minnesota.

TABLE OF CONTENTS

CHAPTER 1

GROUND TROOPS

A Humvee drives through the desert. U.S. Army **Soldiers** are inside! They are ready for action.

U.S. military branch seals

The Army is one **branch** of the U.S. military. All branches **defend** the United States. They also protect U.S. **allies**. The National Guard is part of the military, too. Each state has one.

Some Army Soldiers are pilots. But most are ground **troops**. They often use vehicles. Many of these have **armor** to protect Soldiers. Tanks have weapons on them, too.

M1 Abrams tank

TAKE A LOOK!

The M1 Abrams is the Army's main battle tank. Four Soldiers work inside it. Take a look!

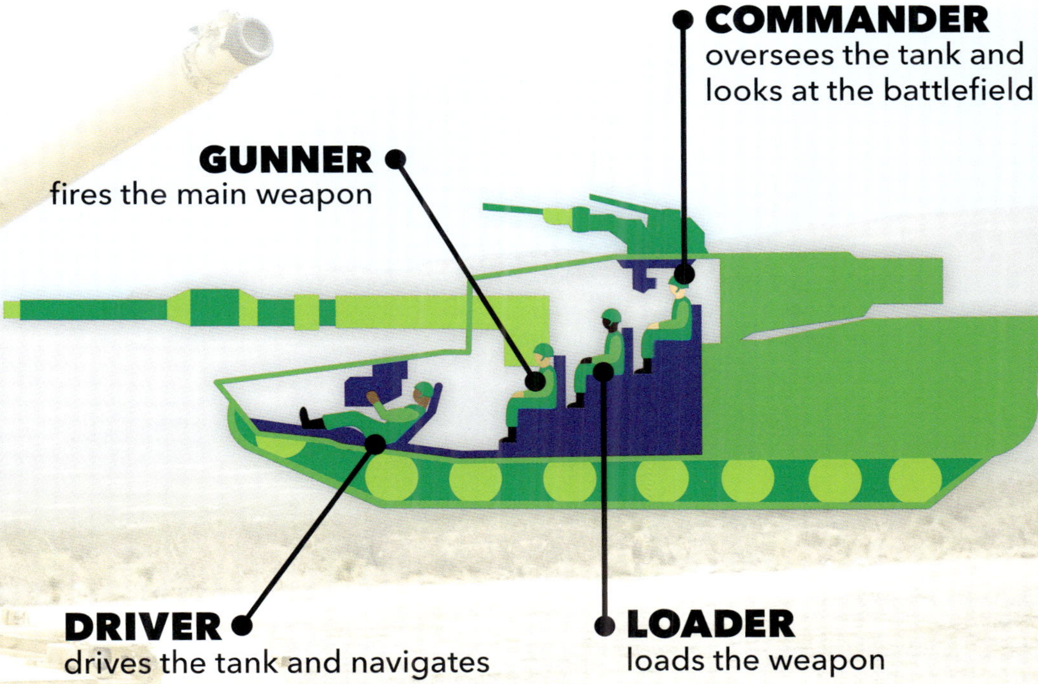

CHAPTER 2

ARMY JOBS

Army **recruits** start with Basic Training. They learn what it takes to be U.S. Soldiers. They must pass physical tests.

After Basic Training, advanced training starts. Soldiers may learn to fire large weapons. Some become computer specialists. Others train to be **engineers**.

After training, each Soldier goes to a **base**. This is where Soldiers live and work. Bases can be in the United States. Or they may be overseas! A Soldier's family can live with him or her on base. Soldiers may move from base to base.

DID YOU KNOW?

Everything Soldiers need is on base. There is a grocery store. It is called a commissary. There is a pool, post office, and gym, too!

COMMISSARY

transport
helicopter
UNITED STATES ARMY

To be an officer, a Soldier must have a college degree. Officers may command a group of Soldiers. Some study to be doctors. Others train to be pilots. They fly **transport** planes or helicopters. They move troops and supplies.

The Army has **special forces**. Rangers are one type. They are ready to go anywhere at any time. They often sneak into enemy **territory**. They may catch enemy troops. Or they may rescue people.

DID YOU KNOW?

The U.S. president is in charge of the U.S. military. He or she decides what the branches will do.

Army Rangers

Green Berets

The Green Berets are another special force. They must have been in the U.S. Army for three years. They fight **terrorists** and collect enemy information. They speak other languages. Sometimes they help train other countries' armies.

WHAT DO YOU THINK?

Night Stalkers are another U.S. Army special force. They are specifically trained to work at night. Would you like to be a Night Stalker? Why or why not?

CHAPTER 3

ARMY MISSIONS

Army **missions** can take place all around the world. Soldiers often join allies in other countries. They work with other U.S. military branches, too. U.S. Navy ships sometimes transport Army troops.

U.S. Navy ships

The U.S. Army Corps of Engineers is a special part of the Army. It helps make rivers safe for boats. It builds locks and **dams**. It also builds military bases.

sandbags

The Army helps during **natural disasters**, too. During a flood, Soldiers build sandbag walls to keep water back. After a hurricane, they bring supplies to those in need.

Army Soldiers protect people around the world. They help them, too! Would you like to serve in the U.S. Army?

WHAT DO YOU THINK?

Army Reserve Soldiers serve part-time. Would you like to serve part-time or full-time? Why?

QUICK FACTS & TOOLS

TIMELINE

1775
The Continental Army is formed during the Revolutionary War (1775–1783).

1777
The Corps of Rangers becomes part of the U.S. Army.

1812–1815
U.S. Army Soldiers defend the United States against the British in the War of 1812.

1941–1945
U.S. Army Soldiers defend European allies from Nazi Germany during World War II (1939–1945).

1952
The Green Berets special operations force is formed.

U.S. ARMY MISSION
The mission of the U.S. Army is to deploy, fight, and win our nation's wars by providing ready, prompt, and sustained land dominance by Army forces across the full spectrum of conflict as part of the joint force.

U.S. ARMY ACTIVE DUTY MEMBERS:
around 475,000 (as of 2019)
Active duty members serve full-time.

U.S. ARMY RESERVE MEMBERS:
around 190,000 (as of 2019)
Reserve members serve part-time.

GLOSSARY

allies: Countries that are on the same side during wars or military actions.

armor: Protective metal plates.

base: A permanent military station.

branch: One of the groups of the U.S. military, including the U.S. Air Force, U.S. Army, U.S. Coast Guard, U.S. Marine Corps, and U.S. Navy.

dams: Barriers across streams or rivers that hold back water.

defend: To protect.

engineers: People who use math and science to solve society's problems and create things that humans use.

missions: Tasks or jobs.

natural disasters: Events in nature, such as hurricanes, earthquakes, and floods, that cause a lot of damage.

recruits: New members of a military force.

Soldiers: People who serve in the Army.

special forces: Specialized military groups that are trained to do particular tasks.

territory: The land and waters under control of a state, nation, or ruler.

terrorists: People who use violence and threats in order to frighten people, obtain power, or force governments to do things.

transport: To carry from place to place.

troops: Members of the armed forces.

INDEX

TO LEARN MORE

Finding more information is as easy as 1, 2, 3.

1. **Go to www.factsurfer.com**
2. **Enter "U.S.Army" into the search box.**
3. **Click the "Surf" button to see a list of websites.**

FACT SURFER